Crave

m. Lee

ISBN: 1466450525
ISBN-13: 9781466450523

DEDICATION

To all those in search of their erotic selves.

CONTENTS

Crescendos

Soft moans and heavy breaths

Crescendos in the night

As we touch each other's love

Minds and bodies, hearts, and souls

Meld into one

We reach the pentacle of desire

Craving satisfied

A Poet's Heart A Poet's Dream

Just in case you were wondering, I haven't been able to forget that last walk on the island. The stones beneath our feet, glistening; washed fresh from the night's rain. Walking silently through the woods down to the shore, you take my hand to steady my steps on the slippery slopes. Waves lap softly against the rocky shoreline scattered with debris brought in from the past week's storms and high tides. In the distance a whale breaches taking our breaths away. Often we see this sight from this very spot at the edge. Always we marvel at the power and grace of the orca; as if we were seeing it for the first time every time. The orca, a metaphor for our love; breaking high out of still waters, splashing down, disappearing into undercurrents. Waves of excitement smoothing out over time leaving no evidence of being.

I want so much for us to work. A poet's dream. I know we will not. A realist's knowing. I wait in silent anguish for your words. The ones I know will prove to be the end.

"I don't think we can do this anymore," you say.

"We," I think. What a surprise. How dare you pretend to know what I can or will do. You have no sense to what lengths I am willing to go. It is you who cannot do this anymore. A poet's heart, my heart, loves forever.

"I know," I whisper. Once again, I acquiesce to you. Accepting your answer to how it will be. Accepting the end of us, but still fighting for more I counter, "It will be some time before I leave. Will you be mine still until that day?"

"Yes, I think that will be good." You give in a little.

With that I have won, I tell myself, a little more time. There is time for you to change your mind; time for you to know that I am what you want; time for you to ask me to stay.

I struggle to tell you, "I will miss you, you know? And this; this beautiful place where we have shared so many private and intimate moments. You know more of me than anyone ever has."

"And you of me. I'm sorry, really sorry. I do love you, but I just can't..."

"I know. It's OK." I tell you with compassion.

I really want to scream and cry, but somewhere deep down I feel your pain, your struggle to commit, and I know you have done your best. I know, even with time your mind, detached from your heart, will not change.

Here I am, a year later, living a country away. I have traveled as far as I can to a place with family and old friends and new friends to be made. I hope that time and space will change me, heal me, give me strength to be different. A year later and...
The ache of a poet's heart, the unreasonableness of a poet's dream, a haiku is all that is left.

a year, it's been hot
opposite side of our world
i still burn for you

The Beginning

Getting to know you
Comfortable with you
Opening up to you

Wanting your touch
Wondering when it will come
Who will reach out first

How unexpected
You loving me
Me loving you

Passion's Delight

Speak to me
of passion's delight
Your lover's words falling softly

Love so wanting, freely given
Blessed agony of desire unmet
Passion's thirst quenched

In a lover's language
Delighting like no other
Moving gently to the rhythm of us

Speak to me

I Dream of You

Wrapped in your arms
Feeling you there

Lost in your grace
Found in your love

All of me
Wanting all of you

My Desire

Morning love

    Soft and gentle

My hand to your sacredness

    My mouth to your passion

I taste your sweetness

    Wandering the whole of you

Your pleasure my desire

To Boundless Ecstasy

Rising up
Inviting my touch
Wanting to fill my hunger
Hands caressing breast's sweet softness
Tongue playing
Soft moans and subtle swaying
Pushing, pulling, guiding
Heat radiating between supple thighs
Arms open wide and holding tight
Sudden gasps
Your wetness against my own
Leg
My belly
My breast
You open to me
A rose in the summer sun
Revealing the center bud
Moving to the rhythm of desire
Taking you beyond
To boundless ecstasy

Your Kiss

Lips full and soft, kissing me
Warm tongue slipping in
Dancing playfully with mine
Lightly at first
Then mouth full open
Hungry for more
Tongue deeply searching
Rushes of joy
Deep between my thighs
Moisture of your mouth
To the moisture of my desire
Tingling, throbbing, aching
Touch me softly, deeply
Harder now, stroking in and out
Like your tongue in my mouth
Dancing with my desire
Hear my moans
Begging for more
Bring to me sweet release
From the blessed agony of waiting
I am yours

No! Maybe! Yes!

I move to hold you close

     "No"

A lick of my tongue

     "Maybe"

A stroke of my finger

     "More"

I part your legs with my own

     "Yes"

You pull me close

     "No"

A lick of your tongue

     "Maybe"

A stroke of your finger

     "More"

Legs intertwined

     "Yes"

Rapture

As I Garden

Thoughts of my lover as I work my garden

Rich soft moist earth lays ready for planting
My fingers dig deeply in

Moist and warm smells of fertility rise up
Like our bed after hours of lovemaking

Each seed planted by design
Tended to just so

Ground warmed by the sun
Kept moist by my hand

Anticipation of things to come
Heightened ecstasy, awaiting garden gifts

Seedlings break through fertile ground
Like my lover's moans break the silence

Growing stronger with each careful touch
Flowers scream forth, multi-colors, sweet scents

Then fall calm into slumber
Resting, waiting for the next spring

Thoughts of my lover as I work my garden

Peach Delight

With orgasmic anticipation I reach for you
Hungering for the softness of your skin
The freshness of your scent
The sweetness of your taste

Taking you in my hands
Pulling you to my face
I breathe you in
Running fingers lightly over the whole of you

I bring your beauty to my mouth
And gently bite
Your juices flow over my tongue
Sucking softly I capture your taste

Ecstasy overcomes me
Your essence trickles down my throat
Hmm, there is nothing like a Georgia Peach
Wouldn't you agree?

Romantic Dinner

Weight of my day melts, you come into view
carefully dressed to thrill
At the table delicacies
meant to be eaten by hand
Lace and china, candles lit
romance simply done
The day will wait, we let it go
enjoy this moment fully
Fingers dance upon each other's
intertwine like our love
Linger as food is sucked off
sounds of joy fall softly around
Falling deeper into each other
souls dancing in delight
Open love, inviting a touch
wanting like no other
No one and nothing more
here in this moment
Save the womyn sitting across the table
passion's warmth glistening
Moving gently to rhythms of love
like all else, the dishes will wait

Vaginas

**A young vagina having lost her virginity
in a most conventional way:**

Really, Really?
That's it?
What is all the hoopla about?
Really, three minutes and it's over?
You just leave me here wet and bruised
and feeling dirty?
I don't get it.
This certainly hasn't been what it was
cracked up to be, no pun intended.
I think I will take a shower.
And the young vagina fell silent.

**A young vagina having lost her virginity
in a less than conventional way:**

Yes! Yes!
Oh yeah baby.
OMG what was I so afraid of.
OMG this is it, this is is is...
Oh yes again, again...
I'm alive.
From the mountain I will shout, "I'm Alive."
Over and over and over again.
And the young vagina's silence was broken.

Written in Braille

Read my body
Your favorite book written in Braille
In the dark your fingers searching
Returning to savor each passage
Adeptly you read each ridge and indentation
Revealing secret plots of ecstasy
Each word building the story of passion
Transporting us to a land before not explored
Read my body
Your favorite book

Crave's *Haikus*

nipples hard as rock
pelvis rises up throbbing
sex, not love making

skin like lavender
passions sweet nectar of love
gentle scent soft touch

dip the strawberry
summer's best love fruit to eat
choc-o-late covered

fall harvest love's food
reaping our adoration
lay on table eat

naked sushi bite
forbidden delight craving
linger on stomach

As We Like It

Toe tickling
Thigh throbbing
Labia licking
Pussy pounding
Cunt crashing
Finger fucking
Sex

ABOUT THE AUTHOR

m. lee lives in the southeastern part of the United States. Her poetry and short stories are inspired by life's experiences, her own and those of others. She has traveled the world in search of new and exciting adventures but admits that the best and most inspiring experiences have always been enjoyed close to home.

Made in the USA
Las Vegas, NV
16 February 2025

18182821R00018